the thing about Dads

This edition copyright © 2001 Lion Publishing
Illustrations copyright © 2001 Graham Cox

Published by
Lion Publishing plc
Sandy Lane West, Oxford, England
www.lion-publishing.co.uk
ISBN 0 7459 4767 0

First edition 2001
10 9 8 7 6 5 4 3 2 1 0

Acknowledgments

49, 74: Colossians 3:21, Matthew 7:9–10, quoted from the Good News
Bible published by The Bible Societies/HarperCollins Publishers Ltd, UK
© American Bible Society 1966, 1971, 1976, 1992, used with permission.

Every effort has been made to trace and acknowledge copyright holders
of all the quotations in this book. We apologize for any errors or omissions
that may remain, and would ask those concerned to contact the publishers,
who will ensure that full acknowledgment is made in the future.

A catalogue record for this book is available
from the British Library

Typeset in Antique Olive Roman
Printed and bound in Malta

the thing about Dads

Compiled by
Olivia Warburton

Illustrated by
Graham Cox

To a one-of-a-kind **dad!**

What dads need

Any man can be a
father, but it takes someone
special to be a dad.

Anne Geddes

A job description

To be a successful father, there's one absolute rule: when you have a kid, don't look at it for the first two years.

Ernest Hemingway

If you can't be kind, at least have the decency to be vague.

Steven Wright

It is a wise father that knows his own child.

William Shakespeare

Parentage is
a very important
profession, but no
test of fitness for it
is ever imposed in
the interest of the
children.

George Bernard Shaw

Dad tries to tidy
my bedroom
as a way of
being helpful,
but I can't
find anything
afterwards.

Colin, 16

12 Before I got married, I had six theories about bringing up children. Now I have six children and no theories.

John Wilmot

> You say 'fatherhood' to me, or 'being a father', I don't have an overall concept of it. It's the best and the worst.
>
> Seb, 39

As a parent,
I do everything
except
breastfeeding.

Andy Gray

He's perfect
just the way he is.

Donovan, 7

Dear
God, my dad
thinks he is you.
Please straighten
him out.

Wayne, 11

It goes without saying
that you should never have
more children than you
have car windows.

Erma Bombeck

Boundless energy

The main purpose of children's parties is to remind you that there are children worse than your own.

Katharine Whitehorn

I would there were no age between ten and three-and-twenty.

William Shakespeare

Children are a kind of discipline of humanity.

Francis Bacon

Even
when freshly washed
and relieved of all obvious
confections, children
tend to be sticky.

Fran Lebowitz

He threw his jelly and
cream all over Dad, then
laughed and clapped.

Adrian Plass

I fed them,
changed their
clothes, washed
them, told them
stories. By noon
each day I was
exhausted.

Henry Miller

I take my children everywhere, but they always find their way home again.

Robert Orben

No animal is so inexhaustible as an excited infant.

Amy Leslie

● ● ● ● ● ● ● ● ● ● ● ● ● ● ● ● ●

Playing with children is a glorious thing, but I have never understood why it is considered a soothing or idyllic one. It reminds me not of watering little budding flowers, but of wrestling for hours with gigantic angels and devils.

G.K. Chesterton

It is admirable for a man to take his son fishing, but there is a special place in heaven for the father who takes his daughter shopping.

John Sinor

● ● ● ● ● ● ● ● ● ● ● ● ● ● ● ● ●

What a dreadful thing it must be to have a dull father.

Mary Mapes Dodge

Some good ideas

It goes with the whole concept of fatherhood — particularly if you've got sons — that dads come into their own with cricket bats and goofing around and building tree houses.

Charles Jennings

The difficult can be done immediately, the impossible takes a little longer.

Army Corps of Engineers

You are always supposed to know,
and if you don't know, you have got to
pretend that you do. If your son asks you
how a combustion engine works, you have
got to cobble something together or
you're not a father.

Geraint, 43

A father decided to tell his young son the facts of life and was stumped right away by the boy's first question: 'How many are there?'

Author unknown

Here is the beginning of understanding: most parents are doing their best, and most children are doing their best, and they're doing pretty well, all things considered.

Richard Louv

I like the way my dad knows all the answers to my homework. And he can play the piano.

Jane, 11

My Dad's my hero. He can kill dragons and do sums and everything.

Fred, 6

Having a family is like having a bowling alley installed in your brain.

Martin Mull

Peace and quiet

I love it when Dad and I are watching TV together on the sofa. Although we always have to watch what he wants, which is normally sport – football mainly.

Emma, 12

After a hard day's work, my dad's idea of bliss was a quiet evening in front of the television with his family – preferably with neither of them making too many demands on him.

Caroline, 20

Anyone who thinks the art of conversation is dead ought to tell a child to go to bed.

Robert Gallagher

Bedtime is the oldest argument in the world.

Juliet Janvrin

Children's volume control is set very high, and they have not yet learned to adjust the sound.

Juliet Janvrin

Beware
the fury of a
patient man.

John Dryden

In every dispute between parent and child, both cannot be right, but they may be, and usually are, both wrong. It is this situation which gives family life its peculiar hysterical charm.

Isaac Rosenfeld

I love sleep. My life has the tendency to fall apart when I'm awake, you know?

Ernest Hemingway

Sometimes the best way to deal with everyday life is to lie down and take a nap.

Joyce Bartels

The secret of dealing
successfully with a child
is not to be its parent.

Mel Lazarus

A little bit of respect

I switch on the TV after a stupid, awkward day and watch it uncritically for an hour and a half. When my children do the same, I nag them and complain that they're wasting their lives.

Charles Jennings

Parents, do not irritate your children, or they will become discouraged.

The Bible

Fathers should be neither seen nor heard. That is the only proper basis for family life.

Oscar Wilde

Children aren't happy
with nothing to ignore,
And that's what
parents were
created for.

Ogden Nash

Go directly – see
what she's doing, and
tell her she mustn't.

Punch, 1872

There's
nothing wrong with
teenagers that reasoning
with them won't aggravate.

Jean Kerr

Parental expressions every child should know:
'Some day you'll thank me' (statement made
by parent who has successfully asserted authority,
in order to soften the victory). 'I don't want to
hear any more about it' (assertion of parental
authority after parent has lost argument with
child).

Judith Martin

I like my dad.
He lets me do
what I want.

Natasha, 7

I have found the best
way to give advice to
your children is to find
out what they want
and then advise them
to do it.

Harry S. Truman

The best way to
keep children home
is to make the home
atmosphere pleasant
– and let the air
out of the tyres.

Dorothy Parker

What kids want is a dad. And dads, by definition, are not cool.

Neil Spencer

Total acceptance

Most of us learn to suppress the child in ourselves. But parents whizz down the playground slide when no one is looking.

Juliet Janvrin

Most of us become parents long before we have stopped being children.

Mignon McLaughlin

Where food is involved, every dad has his little quirks, for which real understanding is required. There is no point debating why he loves marrow but won't eat courgettes, or insists that pancakes are really baps, or why boiled eggs should be decapitated instead of bludgeoned.

Anna-Maria, 25

The thing about dads is... they never quite lose that small-boy-wants-chocolate mentality.

Sophie, 17

Every so often (about once a year), dads feel an overwhelming urge to give ADVICE. Trying to avoid this is as futile as telling a hayfever sufferer not to sneeze.

Robin, 19

Advice for dads:
1. The life children actually live and the life you perceive them to be living is not the same life.
2. Don't keep scorecards on them – a short memory is useful.
3. Don't take what your children do too personally.

Robert Fulghum

Chocolate
is good.
Stodgy puddings
are good.
Vegetables
are not good.

Sarah, 28

Dads fall into two
categories: fit and
not-so-fit. It tends to
be obvious to which
category your own
dad belongs.

Peter, 18

Families are about love overcoming emotional torture.

Matt Groening

Happy families

Every man sees in his relatives a series of grotesque caricatures of himself.

H.L. Mencken

The only thing that prevented a father's love from faltering was the fact that there was in his possession a photograph of himself at the same early age, in which he, too, looked like a homicidal fried egg.

P.G. Wodehouse

The trouble with dads is that their expectation levels can sometimes be set a fraction too high.

Tony Green

A man finds out what is meant by a spitting image when he tries to feed cereal to his infant.

Imogene Fay

Heredity is what a man believes in until his son begins to act like a delinquent.

Author unknown

Your children love you. They want to play with you. How long do you think that will last? We have a few short years with our children when they're the ones that want us around. After that, you'll be running after them for a bit of attention.

Author unknown

The best gift a father can give to his son is the gift of himself – his time. For material things mean little, if there is not someone to share them with.

Neil C. Strait

Would any of you who are fathers give your son a stone when he asks for bread? Or would you give him a snake when he asks for a fish?

The Bible

Success is going from failure to failure without losing enthusiasm.

Winston Churchill

Constant reassurance

When I stop and consider how different they would have been if I hadn't been around, I start to wonder how much of my influence has been good, how much bad, whether they've come out broadly in credit for knowing me, or worse off.

Charles Jennings

The proper time to influence the character of a child is about a hundred years before he is born.

William Ralph Inge

In the final analysis it is not what you do for your children but what you have taught them to do for themselves.

Ann Landers

Parents are sometimes a bit of a disappointment to their children. They don't fulfil the promise of their early years.

Anthony Powell

Allow children to be happy in their own way, for what better way will they find?

Samuel Johnson

Nothing you do for children is ever wasted.
They seem not to notice us, hovering, averting
their eyes, and they seldom offer thanks, but
what we do for them is never wasted.

Garrison Keillor

If you can give your son
or daughter only one gift,
let it be enthusiasm.

Bruce Barton

You will never really know what kind of parent you were or if you did it right or wrong. Never. And you will worry about this and them as long as you live. But when your children have children and you watch them do what they do, you will have part of an answer.

Robert Fulghum

Now there is only the future, and all I do is worry about it. I have panics about things that may happen and things that are relatively unlikely to happen. I panic about them more or less equally.

Charles Jennings

Affection
is responsible for nine-
tenths of whatever solid and
durable happiness there is
in our lives.

C.S. Lewis

Lots of love

If a man smiles at home, somebody is sure to ask him for money.

William Feather

A father is a banker provided by nature.

French proverb

I like my dad because he spends money on me.

Daniel, 12

He opened the jar of pickles when no one else could. He was the only one in the house who wasn't afraid to go into the basement by himself. He cut himself shaving, but no one kissed it or got excited about it. It was understood that when it rained, he got the car and brought it around to the door. When anyone was sick, he went out to get the prescription filled. He took lots of pictures... but he was never in them.

Erma Bombeck

The very words 'my father' make me smile. **91**

Angela Carter

Raising kids is part joy and part guerilla warfare.

Ed Asner

Parenting is not logical. Life is filled with disagreement, opposition, illusion, irrational thinking, miracle, meaning, surprise, and wonder.

Jeanne Elium and Don Elium

I think what is valuable is when you feel appreciated, and parents do that. When I say it's me on the phone, I can tell they are genuinely pleased to hear from me, and that is really special.

Fiona, 27